Women in Conse

T0100828

Dian Fossey
Friend to Africa's Gorillas

Robin S. Doak

Heinemann
LIBRARY
Chicago, Illinois

© 2015 Heinemann Library
an imprint of Capstone Global Library, LLC
Chicago, Illinois
www.capstonepub.com

All rights reserved. No part of this publication may
be reproduced or transmitted in any form or by
any means, electronic or mechanical, including
photocopying, recording, taping, or any information
storage and retrieval system, without permission in
writing from the publisher.

Edited by Clare Lewis, Abby Colich, Diyan Leake,
and Gina Kammer
Designed by Philippa Jenkins
Original illustrations © Capstone Global Library
Ltd 2014

Illustrated by HL Studios p15, Oxford Designers
  and Illustrators p18
Picture research by Tracy Cummins
Production by Victoria Fitzgerald
Originated by Capstone Global Library Ltd

Library of Congress Cataloging-in-Publication Data
Doak, Robin
Dian Fossey: Friend to Africa's Gorillas
(Women in Conservation)

ISBN 978-1-4846-0468-7 (hardcover)
ISBN 978-1-4846-0473-1 (paperback)
ISBN 978-1-4846-0483-0 (eBook PDF)

Acknowledgments
The author and publisher are grateful to the following
for permission to reproduce copyright material:

Alamy: © Ei Katsumata, 6, ©INTERFOTO, 9, © Liam
White, 36, 40, © Moviestore collection Ltd, 13; C.S.
Harcourt: 30; Corbis: © Yann Arthus-Bertrand, 33;
Everett Collection: © Universal, 35; Getty Images: Neil
Selkirk/Time Life Pictures, 34, Photoshot, 17, Robert F.
Sisson/National Geographic, 16, Rodney Brindamour/
National Geographic, 19, Terrence Spencer/Time Life
Pictures, 12; Kosair Charities: 11; National Geographic:
ROBERT I.M. CAMPBELL, 5, 21, 22, 23, 24, 25, 26,
27, 28, 31, 32, front cover; Shutterstock: erwinf, 38,
Matt Trommer, 29, PHOTOCREO Michal Bednarek,
14, PRILL, 4, Sam Chadwick, 43, szefei, design
element, Tyler Olson, 8; The Dian Fossey Gorilla Fund
International: 800 Cherokee Ave. SE, Atlanta, GA
30315, ph. 1-800-851-0203, 7; University of Louisville:
Ekstrom Library/Archives and Special Collections, 10

We would like to thank Michael Bright for his
invaluable help in the preparation of this book.

Every effort has been made to contact copyright
holders of any material reproduced in this book. Any
omissions will be rectified in subsequent printings if
notice is given to the publisher.

All the Internet addresses (URLs) given in this book
were valid at the time of going to press. However, due
to the dynamic nature of the Internet, some addresses
may have changed, or sites may have changed or
ceased to exist since publication. While the author and
publisher regret any inconvenience this may cause
readers, no responsibility for any such changes can be
accepted by either the author or the publisher.

Contents

Some words are printed in bold, **like this**. You can find out
what they mean by looking in the glossary on page 45.

Who Was Dian Fossey?

Dian Fossey was 34 years old when she left her home and job in Kentucky and moved to Africa. She spent the next 19 years studying mountain gorillas, an **endangered species**. She devoted her life to researching these mysterious creatures, which are some of humankind's closest relatives.

Each day Fossey trekked into the mountains of Rwanda. She spent hours sitting and observing the animals' behaviors. Over time the gorillas came to trust and even accept her. She developed strong bonds with a number of the animals and cared deeply about all of them.

The **rain forests** of the Virunga Mountains are home to the endangered mountain gorilla.

Dian Fossey brought international attention to mountain gorillas.

Educating humans, saving gorillas

Fossey's research led to increased knowledge about mountain gorillas. She uncovered many new facts about these gentle giants. She brought the gorillas to the attention of the world. Thanks to Fossey, people all over the globe came to know the gorillas she had named Digit, Peanuts, and Uncle Bert. And just like her, people came to care deeply about whether these animals lived or died.

Fossey was not afraid to make enemies to protect her gorillas. She waged war against those who tried to harm the animals. In the end, her **aggressive** methods led to her death. But Fossey's work did not die with her. Today people around the world still work to make sure that gorillas do not become **extinct**.

DID YOU KNOW?

- There are just two species of gorillas in the world: eastern gorillas and western gorillas. Mountain gorillas fall within the eastern gorilla group.
- Gorillas, chimps, orangutans, and bonobos are **great apes**, humankind's closest living relatives.
- Male mountain gorillas can grow to be up to 485 pounds (220 kilograms) and 5 feet, 6 inches (168 centimeters) tall when standing upright.

What Was Fossey's Early Life Like?

Dian Fossey was born on January 16, 1932, in San Francisco, California. Her mother, Hazel, known as Kitty, was a former model. Her father, George, was an insurance agent.

Dian's parents divorced when she was a young girl, and George disappeared from his daughter's life. She would not see him again for 30 years. Kitty Fossey then married a wealthy businessman named Richard Price.

As an adult, Dian visited her parents in California where she grew up.

(The Dian Fossey Gorilla Fund International)

Dian was a tall, intelligent child who adored animals of all kinds.

Shy and studious as a girl, Dian always felt awkward and ashamed of her height. By the time she was 14, she had grown to be nearly 6 feet (183 centimeters) tall. She got little support or encouragement from her mother. Dian would later remember her childhood with anger and sadness.

A friend in animals

An only child who longed for love and affection, Dian turned her attention to animals. At age 6, she began horse-riding lessons. Horses and other animals soon became the center of her world. As she grew older, when she was not busy studying, Dian was often riding horses.

In her own words

Dian told friends that her parents would not let her have cats, dogs, or other furry pets in the house. But she was allowed to have a goldfish. She remembered:

> "I cried for a week when I found him floating belly up in the bowl in my room."

A classmate offered her a guinea pig, but her parents refused.

Choosing a career

Dian graduated from high school in 1949. She signed up as a **veterinary science** major at the University of California at Davis. Unfortunately, Dian struggled with **physics** and **chemistry**, two courses required for future veterinarians. She flunked out of college in her second year.

What would Dian do now? She could not follow her heart and become a veterinarian. But she still wanted to help those who could not help themselves. She turned her focus to children in need.

Helping others

Dian transferred to San Jose State College and studied **occupational therapy**. An occupational therapist helps people with physical or other disabilities learn how to lead independent, meaningful lives. Dian hoped to help disabled children by teaching them crafts and other skills. She graduated in 1954.

Dian graduated from San Jose State College in 1954.

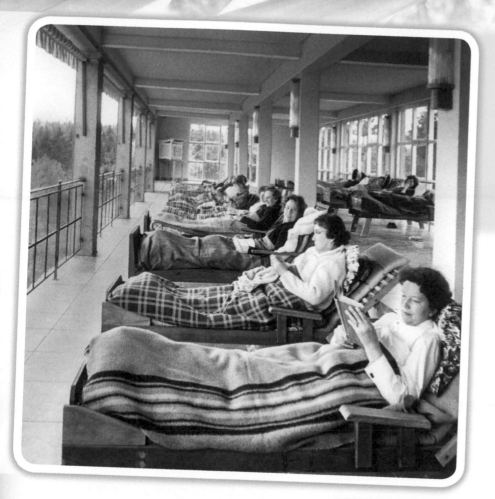

During the 1950s, better medicines and treatment reduced the number of people suffering from tuberculosis.

After college, Dian worked as an intern (student receiving training) at a number of California hospitals. At one hospital, she helped patients suffering from tuberculosis, a serious disease affecting the lungs. Although she enjoyed this work, Dian wanted to leave California and explore other parts of the country. When she saw a "help wanted" ad for an occupational therapist in Louisville, Kentucky, she immediately applied.

DID YOU KNOW?

When Dian was 19, she took a summer job at a horse ranch in Montana. Here she could do what she loved—ride horses all day long. The job came to an unexpected end when Dian developed chicken pox and had to quit. Her time at the ranch was one of her favorite memories.

A home in Kentucky

In fall 1955, Dian Fossey arrived in Louisville, Kentucky. She would spend the next eight years there, serving as the director of occupational therapy at the Kosair Crippled Children Hospital. The hospital helped children who had difficulties walking.

Away from the hospital, Fossey rented a small cottage on an isolated farm. She was free to spend time with animals there. She helped the farm's owner tend his livestock and collected stray dogs as pets. She also continued riding horses.

Fossey worked at the Kosair Crippled Children Hospital in Louisville, Kentucky, for eight years.

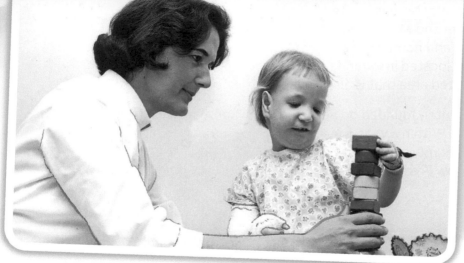

Fossey helps a child at the Kosair Crippled Children Hospital.

(Kosair Charities)

Making a difference

At the Kosair Crippled Children Hospital, Fossey earned a reputation as someone who worked hard and had a special way with kids. She did not talk down to them or baby them. Her patients seemed to sense that she truly cared about their health and well-being.

Fossey had a harder time bonding with her coworkers. She never seemed to have time to chat, and she did not attend get-togethers outside the office. Some said that Fossey seemed to prefer the company of animals.

Fossey did make one strong friendship at Kosair. An outgoing woman named Mary White Henry shared an office with Fossey. The Louisville native also worked at a travel agency and had visited many places around the world. When she vacationed in Africa, she invited her new friend to come along. Unfortunately, Fossey could not afford the trip.

The Henry family

In Kentucky, Fossey found the family that she longed for. Mary White Henry's family embraced Fossey as one of their own. Fossey was especially close to Mary's mother, Gaynee. Before long, Mary and her sister nicknamed Fossey "Mother's other daughter."

Learning about gorillas

In 1963 Fossey decided to make a bold move. She used her life savings along with an $8,000 loan to plan a trip to eastern Africa. Fossey hoped to pay the money back by selling stories and photos of her adventure to newspapers and magazines.

During her upcoming seven-week trip, Fossey planned to visit the wild animals of Africa in their natural **habitats**. She wrote: "I had a deep wish to see and live with wild animals in a world that hadn't been completely changed by humans."

George Schaller spent 20 months observing mountain gorillas in the Virunga volcanoes of Central Africa.

The ape in the movie *King Kong* gave gorillas a bad name.

The animal that she was most interested in was the mountain gorilla, one of the largest **primates** in the world. After her trip to Africa, Fossey had read *The Year of the Gorilla* by scientist George Schaller. She was fascinated by Schaller's descriptions of the animals and wanted to go back.

DID YOU KNOW?

Before Fossey's research, gorillas had a bad reputation. Most people associated them with the angry, aggressive animal depicted in the movie *King Kong*. These huge animals were known to charge at humans. Frightened Africans often shot gorillas on sight.

George Shaller

George Schaller, an American expert in **zoology**, was one of the first scientists to study mountain gorillas. In 1959 he set up camp in the Belgian Congo and began observing the misunderstood creatures. Schaller was forced to end his research in 1960, when war erupted in the region. He later wrote: "No one who looks into a gorilla's eyes—intelligent, gentle, vulnerable—can remain unchanged."

What Were Fossey's Early Trips to Africa Like?

On September 26, 1963, Fossey first left the United States for Africa. Her gear included a 44-pound (20-kilogram) chest of medicines to treat her **asthma** as well as any other illnesses she might develop. She also brought along a new pair of good boots and some bug repellant.

In Nairobi, the capital of Kenya, Fossey met up with her guide. John Alexander was a British man who had been leading tourists on hunting safaris for many years. Although Fossey did not want to hunt, Alexander's knowledge of where the animals were made him the perfect guide.

Fossey fell in love with Africa's rugged terrain.

The trip of a lifetime

The pair set off in Alexander's off-road vehicle. One of their first stops was the Serengeti Plains, located in Kenya and Tanzania. The Serengeti is known as one of the seven natural wonders of the world. Twice each year, hundreds of thousands of wildebeests (a kind of antelope), zebras, and other animals travel 500 miles (800 kilometers) across the plains.

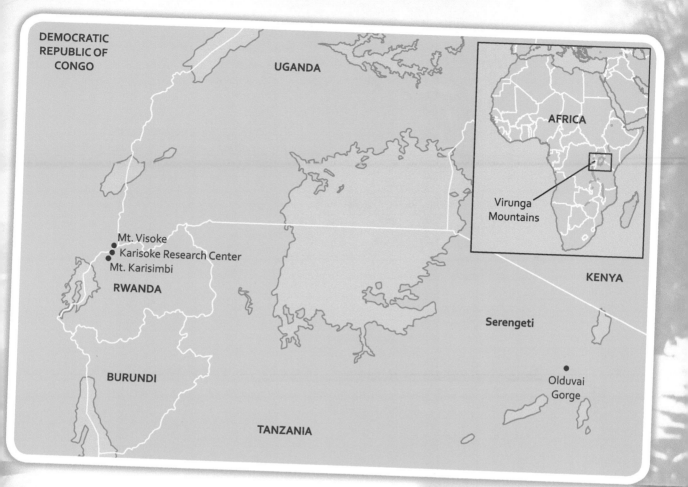

DEMOCRATIC
REPUBLIC OF
CONGO

UGANDA

AFRICA

Virunga
Mountains

Mt. Visoke
Karisoke Research Center
Mt. Karisimbi

RWANDA

KENYA

Serengeti

BURUNDI

Olduvai
Gorge

TANZANIA

Every day Fossey took dozens of photos. Each night she wrote in her journal about the day's events. But there was growing tension between Fossey and her guide. Alexander would later remember his client as grumpy and difficult. The trip continued, and the experienced hunter took Fossey wherever she wanted to go. One important goal of the trip was for Fossey to meet the famed scientist Louis Leakey.

Fossey's tour of eastern Africa took her through several countries, including Kenya, Tanganyika (now part of Tanzania), and the Congo.

Meeting a legend

In 1963 scientist Louis Leakey was famous in the fields of **archaeology** and **paleontology**. Just three years earlier, Leakey and his wife, Mary, had discovered important **fossils** at Olduvai **Gorge** in Tanzania. The remains proved that humans were much older than previously believed.

Fossey visited Olduvai Gorge with her guide. Leakey was excited when he heard that Fossey intended to look for mountain gorillas in the Congo. He talked to her about Jane Goodall, a young woman who was doing a long-term study of chimpanzees in Tanzania. Finally Leakey told Fossey to keep in touch. This visit was short, but it had a lasting impact on her.

Together Louis and Mary Leakey made groundbreaking discoveries in East Africa.

Joan and Alan Root were working on a documentary film about mountain gorillas when they met Fossey.

First contact

Fossey had saved her most exciting stop for last. She and Alexander now headed into the Virunga Mountains, home of Africa's mountain gorillas. They stopped at Kabara, a meadow in the Congo where George Schaller had once made his camp. Here Fossey met wildlife photographers Joan and Alan Root. The husband and wife team agreed to take the visiting American woman with them into the mountains.

The trip into the misty, thickly forested mountains was life-changing for Fossey. After seeing the magnificent animals, she was fascinated. She later said that she knew she would somehow return to study the amazing creatures she had seen.

In her own words

Here's how Fossey described her first contact with gorillas:

"Sound preceded sight. Odor preceded sound ... The air was suddenly [disturbed] by a high-pitched series of screams ...Peeking through the **vegetation** we could distinguish an equally curious [group] of black, leather-countenanced, furry-headed primates peering back at us. I was struck by the physical magnificence of the huge jet-black bodies."

An opportunity

After seven weeks touring East Africa, Fossey reluctantly returned to her job and home in Kentucky. Life continued as usual, but Africa and the gorillas remained in her heart.

When Fossey left Africa, she did not know that one of Louis Leakey's dreams was to conduct studies of three great ape species: chimpanzees, gorillas, and orangutans. Leakey had already picked Jane Goodall to research chimpanzees. Now he was keeping an eye out for someone to travel to Africa and conduct a long-term study of mountain gorillas. Years later he would choose Biruté Galdikas to study orangutans.

Fossey's studies of gorillas showed her that they have unique personalities similar to humans.

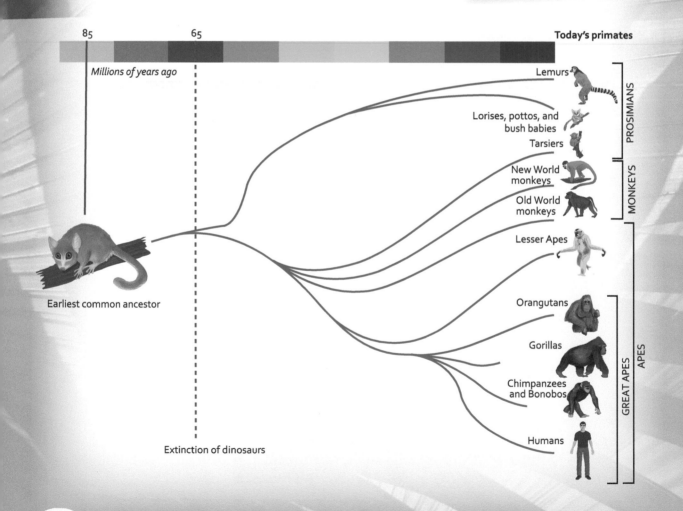

85   65   Today's primates

Millions of years ago

Lemurs — PROSIMIANS

Lorises, pottos, and bush babies

Tarsiers

New World monkeys — MONKEYS

Old World monkeys

Lesser Apes

Earliest common ancestor

Orangutans

Gorillas — GREAT APES — APES

Chimpanzees and Bonobos

Extinction of dinosaurs

Humans

Biruté Galdikas also worked with Leakey. She began researching orangutans in 1971.

In April 1966 Leakey visited Louisville to give a lecture and Fossey reconnected with the famed scientist. Leakey talked about his dream of studying mountain gorillas. At this time, only about 240 of these creatures remained. Leakey wanted to learn about the animals before they became extinct.

DID YOU KNOW?
Mountain gorillas are one of four **subspecies** of gorilla. The other three are the eastern lowland gorilla (called Grauer's gorilla), the western lowland gorilla, and the cross river gorilla.

Leakey was impressed with the articles Fossey had written after her trip. He asked her to be his "gorilla girl." Fossey jumped at the chance to return to the Virunga Mountains. Because the study was funded, she did not have to worry about raising money for the trip.

Home to Africa

Although her family and friends were against the move, 34-year-old Fossey quit her job in Kentucky and flew to Kenya in December 1966. One of her first visits was to Jane Goodall's research camp in Tanzania. Here Goodall showed Leakey's new researcher how to collect data (information and facts) and set up a camp. Fossey also met Goodall's chimpanzees.

Kidnapping and a new camp

By January 1967, Fossey had set up a camp at Kabara in the Congo. Each day for six months, she climbed into the cold, wet rain forests of the Virungas to watch the big apes. But life in the Congo could be dangerous. Different groups of native people were battling each other for control. On July 9, 1967, Fossey was forced from her camp by armed soldiers. She was held captive for two weeks before she managed to escape.

Being kidnapped in a distant country would have sent most people flying home on the next airplane. But Dian Fossey was different. She decided that she would leave the Congo and make her camp in the part of the Virungas in Rwanda. Fossey purchased new equipment for her second camp and prepared to start over.

DID YOU KNOW?

When Fossey began her research in Rwanda, mountain gorillas were in serious danger. Farmers let herds of cattle roam the gorillas' habitat. Cattle destroyed the land and vegetation the gorillas needed to survive. **Poachers** illegally hunting antelopes in the forests sometimes caught gorillas in their traps. Trapped gorillas often died from their injuries or were killed by the poachers.

The Karisoke Research Center

Fossey's new campsite was located between two extinct volcanoes, Mount Karisimbi and Mount Visoke. She combined the names of the two mountains and named her camp the Karisoke Research Center. The center was located in Rwanda, in Volcanoes National Park. The park is a protected area that is also shared by the Congo and Uganda.

The research center, founded on September 24, 1967, started off as two small tents. Within a year, friends helped Fossey build a small cabin. It gave her more space to live and work comfortably. Karisoke was now Fossey's home.

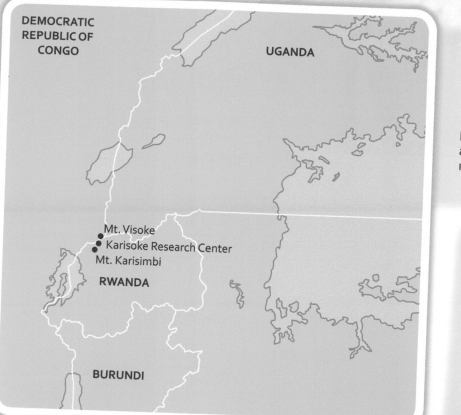

DEMOCRATIC
REPUBLIC OF
CONGO

UGANDA

Mt. Visoke
Karisoke Research Center
Mt. Karisimbi

RWANDA

BURUNDI

Fossey spent 18 years at Karisoke studying mountain gorillas.

Fossey's Karisoke was completely destroyed during the wars that tore Rwanda apart in the 1990s. It has since been reopened at a new site.

How Did Fossey Study Gorillas?

When she founded Karisoke, Dian Fossey had no formal training in how to study wild animals. She was not a scientist, and she had never done research before. She had no experts with her at the center whom she could ask for help.

Fossey soon developed her own research methods. At first, she followed the advice recommended by most animal experts: to be quiet and observe. Every morning, she grabbed a backpack, binoculars, and notebook and set out to make the long, steep climb up into gorilla territory. She sat for hours, hidden by the thick forest vegetation, just watching the gorillas and taking notes.

Fossey created thousands of pages of notes during her first few years researching the gorillas.

Fossey was the first researcher to get close to a mountain gorilla.

Making gorilla friends

Fossey suspected that the gorillas would never behave naturally unless they became used to her presence. She decided that she would have to convince the gorillas that she was not a threat. But how could she do this?

Fossey tried a new approach. To put the animals at ease, she began imitating their behaviors. She groomed herself, thumped on her chest, and walked on her knuckles like the big apes. She even taught herself to make gorilla noises. Soon the gorillas were curiously watching Fossey as she tried to fit in.

Gorilla talk

Fossey had names for many of the sounds the gorillas made. For example, "pig grunts" were noises the animals made to settle a fight or punish a naughty youngster. The "hoot bark" was heard when the gorillas were curious or frightened. She nicknamed many other sounds, including "belch" noises and "wraagh" noises. It took Fossey some time to learn to "speak" the gorillas' language.

Learning about gorilla groups

Fossey learned that mountain gorillas live together in social units of up to 20 animals. An adult male gorilla known as a silverback is a group's leader. Eventually Fossey chose to focus on four groups of gorillas—groups 4, 5, 8, and 9. There were 51 total animals in these groups when she started.

Fossey learned that each gorilla had its own unique personality. To help her quickly identify them, she gave the gorillas names that she thought suited them. These names included Icarus, Old Goat, Beethoven, and Puck. She even named gorillas after some of her family: Uncle Bert and Flossie were named after beloved relatives in California.

Fossey imitates Peanuts as he scratches himself.

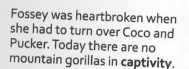

Fossey was heartbroken when she had to turn over Coco and Pucker. Today there are no mountain gorillas in **captivity**.

Gaining fame—and criticism

Fossey's studies and her courage in staying alone in the rain forest earned her international attention. In 1968 the National Geographic Society began funding her research. She also received offers to leave Africa to give lectures on her findings.

Not all people agreed with Fossey's methods. Some believed that naming the gorillas was bad science. They felt that Fossey mistakenly treated the gorillas as if they were humans. And some people felt that it was ridiculous for her to imitate gorilla behavior. She was there to study the animals, they said, not to interact with them.

DID YOU KNOW?

In 1969 two young gorillas were captured by poachers. The gorillas, Coco and Pucker, were destined for a zoo in Germany. But both babies became very sick. Someone from a local park gave them to Fossey in the hopes she might save them. She turned her cabin into a mini–rain forest and nursed them back to health. The animals were taken from her, and they died nine years later in a zoo.

Important progress

During Fossey's first years with mountain gorillas, she made many important discoveries about their behavior. Although initially untrained, she became the top mountain gorilla expert in the world.

Fossey also made progress in recovering some of the gorillas' natural habitat. She and the men she had hired to work with her drove most of the cows out of the area. The gorillas had more room to roam. Fossey also taught her helpers how to destroy the traps that poachers set in the park. The farmers and poachers were very upset about Fossey's actions.

The first gorilla to touch Fossey was Peanuts, a young adult male.

Fossey sometimes broke her own rule of never touching a gorilla after she learned the animals enjoyed being tickled.

In her own words

Fossey often described her interaction with Peanuts as one of the most rewarding parts of her time among the gorillas. Peanuts may have felt the same way. She wrote about the time they touched hands, saying:

> "Thrilled at his own daring, he gave vent to his excitement by a quick chestbeat before going off to rejoin his group. Since that day, the spot has been called...'the Place of the Hands.'"

Close contact

In her first year at Karisoke, Fossey managed to come within 20 feet (6 meters) of the group of gorillas known as Group 5, led by a gorilla she called Beethoven. Then, in 1970, a Group 8 gorilla that she called Peanuts touched her hand. The moment was bittersweet for Fossey. The next day, she was leaving the jungle for seven months to study at a college in England.

Bob Campbell

In 1968 the National Geographic Society sent Bob Campbell to Rwanda to photograph and film Fossey and her gorillas. Campbell was a British photographer who had made a name for himself photographing animals in Africa. After his assignment with Fossey, he went on to become a cameraman on a British nature show called *Survival*. Today he lives in Kenya.

Changing a negative image

In her first three years in Africa, Dian Fossey spent more than 2,000 hours observing mountain gorillas. She had hundreds of pages of notes and was able to give people a different picture of gorillas. Instead of being angry, aggressive beasts, she described them as shy, peaceful, plant eaters that are gentle giants. Leakey proudly wrote to Fossey's parents, saying: "She will achieve an outstanding place in the scientific world by the time she has finished."

Most people around the world first heard of Dian Fossey when she appeared on the cover of *National Geographic*.

DID YOU KNOW?

In January 1970, a photo of Fossey and two gorilla babies appeared on the cover of *National Geographic* magazine. The story inside discussed Fossey's work at Karisoke. People everywhere began to take an interest in the fate of the mountain gorilla. As a result, Fossey had more success at raising funds for her center.

Fossey missed her gorillas when she was at the University of Cambridge.

In 1970 Fossey flew to England and went to the University of Cambridge to continue her education. In the coming years, she traveled between Europe and Africa, spending as much time with her gorillas as possible. While at Cambridge, she wrote an important paper on the behavior of mountain gorillas. In 1974 she earned a doctorate in zoology from the university. A doctorate is the highest degree given by colleges and universities.

Gorilla prints

At Karisoke, Fossey discovered that no two gorillas have the same nose print. The patterns of wrinkles on the nose help researchers identify individual gorillas—just like humans are identified by their unique fingerprints. Fossey also found that a gorilla's nose print changes over time. Today workers at Karisoke make sure they frequently update each gorilla's file with any changes.

Why Did Fossey Return to Africa?

In 1974 Fossey returned to live full time in Rwanda. Her goal was to take a **census** of the region's gorilla **population**. She wanted to prove that poachers and **deforestation** were causing the gorillas to die out. And now, Fossey had more help with her project. A number of college students arrived at Karisoke to work with and learn from the gorilla expert.

Fossey's first step was to train the young volunteers to properly approach the gorillas. She taught them her methods of making the animals comfortable. She warned them never to run from a charging gorilla. Fossey also expected her students to help her destroy traps and confront poachers. Many volunteers were unhappy doing these activities.

As Fossey struggled with her health, her students did more and more of the physical work. These students included Alexander Harcourt (left) and Kelly Stewart (right).

Alexander Harcourt

One of the students who worked for Fossey was Alexander "Sandy" Harcourt. He spent more than three years at Karisoke. During that time, he developed his own ideas about gorilla **conservation**. He and another Fossey student, Kelly Stewart, later married and helped found the Mountain Gorilla Project. Their group involved local Rwandans in saving gorillas.

Fossey angered local hunters by destroying their traps.

Health problems

Help came at a good time for Fossey. She suffered from asthma and had experienced several episodes of **pneumonia**. She also had problems with her legs and feet. As time passed, Fossey found it harder and harder to climb into the mountains to visit the gorillas.

When Fossey was sick or unhappy, she could be difficult to work with. She had a short temper and preferred to be left alone. She was often unkind to students who came to Africa to help her. Few students stayed long at Karisoke. One former volunteer said: "[Animals] took the place of humans, because Dian couldn't deal with humans."

"My beloved Digit"

Fossey had a special bond with a gorilla from Group 4 that she named Digit. For 10 years, she watched Digit grow into a strong, handsome silverback. With his expressive eyes and playful manner, he quickly became her favorite.

Digit interacted with Fossey more than any other gorilla. He would often pat her head or fall asleep at her side. He would also let Fossey tickle him, and the pair would play together. Those who knew the scientist said that Digit was almost like a child to her.

Fossey had a strong connection with a gorilla named Digit.

Digit was buried alongside other gorillas who had lost their lives to poachers.

Digit's death

On December 31, 1977, Digit was killed by poachers while defending the rest of his group from capture and death. The poachers cut off Digit's head and hands for trophies and left his body in the jungle.

An enraged Fossey declared war against the poachers. She organized **patrols** and forced her students to take part. They invaded nearby villages and took people back to Karisoke against their will. Her choices drew strong criticism and angered many people.

Many **conservationists** also challenged Fossey's methods of helping the gorillas. Some believed that the best way to help gorillas (and other endangered animals) was to win the goodwill and cooperation of the local people. Today Rwanda's gorilla **tourism industry** is based on this plan. This type of conservation is considered the best hope for the mountain gorilla's survival.

In her own words

Fossey later wrote about how she felt when she heard of Digit's death. She said:

"All of Digit's life, since my first meeting with him as a playful little ball of fluff 10 years earlier, passed through my mind. From that moment on, I came to live within an insulated [separate or protected] part of myself."

Making headlines, raising awareness

A heartbroken Fossey took her case against the poachers to the public. People in the United States were horrified when the well-known gorilla's death was reported on the evening news. In June 1978, Fossey founded the Digit Fund to honor her friend and raise money to protect mountain gorillas.

But headlines and money were not enough to save the gorillas. The gorillas called Uncle Bert and Macho were killed by poachers. Their baby, Kweli, died later from a bullet wound he received in the same attack. The three animals were buried near Digit in the gorilla graveyard.

Fossey spent more and more time alone in her cabin. Many people said that she had "gone bushy," meaning she had spent too much time alone in the rain forest.

Fossey spent three years as a visiting associate professor at Cornell University.

SIGOURNEY WEAVER · BRYAN BROWN

In a land of beauty, wonder and danger, she would follow a dream, fall in love and risk her life to save the mountain gorillas from extinction.

The true adventure of Dian Fossey.

GORILLAS IN THE MIST

The movie *Gorillas in the Mist* was shown in movie theaters around the world.

Return to the United States

In 1980 Fossey left Africa to become a visiting associate professor at Cornell University in Ithaca, New York. During her stay in the United States, she finished work on the book she had begun years before, called *Gorillas in the Mist*. The book, published in 1983, became an instant **best seller**, read by millions of people. It described Fossey's years of research and the deep bonds she had forged with the animals. The book was dedicated to the gorilla friends she had lost to poacher violence.

DID YOU KNOW?

Gorillas in the Mist was made into a movie in 1988. The movie, which starred Sigourney Weaver, was a hit. It helped spark a new tourism industry in Rwanda. The nation benefited from the money earned as visitors traveled to Africa to visit the gorillas they had seen in the movie.

35

Was Fossey in Danger?

In the United States, Fossey finally had time to take care of herself. Her health got better, and she seemed to regain some of her spirit and energy. She got in touch with some old friends. She even joined Leakey's other ape researchers, Jane Goodall and Biruté Galdikas, at speaking events.

Fossey spent the last year and a half of her life at Karisoke.

Karisoke was forever on Fossey's mind. When she heard reports that more gorillas were being hunted and killed by poachers, she knew she had to return. In the summer of 1983, Fossey would travel to Africa for the last time. One of the first things she did was go into the mountains to find the gorillas.

Things fall apart

Back at Karisoke, Fossey once again went on the attack against poachers. When her men captured a poacher, she may have pretended that she was going to harm the man. As these and other stories leaked out, Fossey lost funding for her center.

Some Rwandans had also tired of Fossey. In trying to save her gorillas, she made a number of dangerous local enemies. Politicians worried that her rough manners kept tourists away from the gorillas. She began receiving death threats and warnings. Fossey even suspected that her pet gray parrots had been poisoned.

In her own words

Fossey described her first meeting with Group 5 after returning to Africa in 1983. She wrote:

"They really did KNOW me immediately after staring into my face ... then [resting] all on top of me and around me ... I could have died right then and wished for nothing more on earth simply because they remembered."

A tragic ending

Before sunrise on December 27, 1985, someone broke into Fossey's cabin at Karisoke and brutally murdered her. At her funeral, she was buried next to Digit, the gorilla she had loved so much. The wooden marker placed on her grave had the name Rwandans called her: "Nyiramachabelli." Fossey said that it meant "She who lives in the forest alone." The plaque placed beneath it reads: "No one loved gorillas more."

Dian Fossey was buried in the gorilla graveyard, alongside 17 gorillas, her pet monkey, and her dog.

In her own words

The last words that Dian Fossey wrote in her journal were:

"When you realize the value of all life, you dwell less on what is past and concentrate more on the **preservation** of the future."

Today the mystery of who killed Dian Fossey remains. Most people believed that Fossey was murdered by poachers. Many people were surprised when one of her student volunteers was charged with the crime. A second man whom Fossey had recently fired was also charged. Although both men were found guilty by Rwandan juries, many people do not consider either of them to be the true killer.

DID YOU KNOW?

One of the prime suspects in Fossey's murder is a former Rwandan politician known as "Mr. Z." He has never been charged with Fossey's murder, but many believed that he ordered the scientist's death. In 2008 he was found guilty of war crimes. Later, however, Mr. Z was released from jail because of mistakes made during his trial.

Honoring the memory of "Nyiramachabelli"

After Fossey's death, the Digit Fund was renamed the Dian Fossey Gorilla Fund International. The group remains active today. It carries on Fossey's mission to save mountain gorillas and educate the world about these gentle giants.

Dian Fossey's **legacy** is the survival of one of the world's most endangered species.

Fossey would be proud of her foundation. It is still considered the world's most important facility for studying the mountain gorilla. It works to protect not only mountain gorillas in the Virungas, but also other endangered species found there. The group's work has expanded to care for another species of gorilla, the eastern lowland gorilla found in the Congo.

New ways to help animals

Over the years, the group has tried new approaches to save gorillas. Now the group works directly with native people to help them preserve the gorillas' habitat. It also funds other groups that help Rwandans living near gorilla territory. These groups help Rwandans find ways to make a living that do not endanger the gorillas' habitat.

Karisoke still exists, although things have changed. Beginning in 1990, Rwanda was torn apart by war. During that time, Fossey's original camp was destroyed. Her cabin was burned to the ground. But by 1998 the Gorilla Fund had set up a new center. The work continues.

Keeping gorillas alive

How would Fossey feel about her Gorilla Fund encouraging tourists to visit the Virungas? The fund's director, Veronica Vecellio, says: "I'm sure that if she was still there now, she would just appreciate the fact that thanks to the tourists, the gorilla [gets] to be alive. Before it was her keeping the gorillas alive, and now it's the tourism."

What Impact Did Fossey's Work Have on Animal Conservation Causes?

Dian Fossey was a **controversial** figure. Some scientists criticized her methods of study. Other people disliked her strong personality. During her 18 years in Africa, she made many enemies. But no matter what she did or said, Fossey always had one key goal in mind: to protect and preserve mountain gorillas in Africa.

Fossey was successful. Her observations and writings raised awareness of this mysterious endangered species. Her research changed the way people thought about the animals by showing that they were gentle, intelligent creatures. Thanks to Fossey's efforts, there are now about 700 mountain gorillas living in the Virunga Mountains. Some of them are animals that Fossey herself studied and loved.

Who will save the gorillas?

Rwandans rely on mountain gorillas to bring tourists to their country. Right now, tourism is Rwanda's top source of income. The image of a gorilla even appears on the country's money. Uganda and the Congo are also taking advantage of gorilla tourism.

Fossey dedicated her entire life to the mountain gorilla, and she eventually made the ultimate sacrifice. But others have picked up where she left off, and the fight to save the mountain gorilla from becoming extinct continues. Why did Dian Fossey fight so hard for the mountain gorilla? She once told a reporter: "When I look at a gorilla, I feel like I'm looking at the better part of myself."

DID YOU KNOW?

- The gorillas of Volcanoes National Park in Rwanda are the only great ape population to have grown in number in recent years.
- Thanks to Fossey's long-term study, scientists have recently learned that the life span (average age lived) of a mountain gorilla is about 35 years.
- The Gorilla Fund helps gorillas that are rescued from poachers return to the wild.

Mountain gorillas still
need our protection.

Timeline

1932   Dian Fossey is born on January 16, 1932, in San Francisco, California

1949   Fossey graduates from high school and begins to study veterinary science at the University of California at Davis

1954   Fossey graduates from San Jose State College with a degree in occupational therapy

1955   Fossey becomes the director of occupational therapy at the Kosair Crippled Children Hospital in Louisville, Kentucky

1963   Fossey travels to Africa for a seven-week vacation. During the trip, she meets Dr. Louis Leakey and sees her first mountain gorillas.

1966   APRIL: During a visit to Louisville, Leakey asks Fossey if she would like to study mountain gorillas
DECEMBER: Fossey arrives in Africa to begin her groundbreaking studies

1967   JANUARY: Fossey sets up her first research camp in the Congo
JULY: She is forced to abandon the camp
SEPTEMBER 24: Fossey founds the Karisoke Research Center in Rwanda

1968   The National Geographic Society begins funding Fossey's research

1969   Fossey nurses Coco and Pucker, two orphaned gorillas, back to health

1970   In January Fossey appears on the cover of *National Geographic* magazine. A gorilla named Peanuts touches Fossey's hand. Fossey leaves Karisoke to earn a doctorate from the University of Cambridge, in England

1974   Fossey returns to live in Rwanda and take a census of the gorilla population there

1977   Digit is killed by poachers

1978   Fossey founds the Digit Fund

1980   Fossey begins a three-year assignment as a visiting associate professor at Cornell University, in Ithaca, New York

1983   *Gorillas in the Mist* is published. Fossey travels back to Africa and Karisoke

1985   Fossey is murdered in her cabin in December

Glossary

aggressive active and energetic

archaeology study of ancient people and the way they lived

asthma health condition that can cause severe breathing difficulties

best seller book that sells a large number of copies

captivity being held in confinement; not free

census official count of the number of animals or people in an area

chemistry science that deals with elements (the basic substances from which all things are made) and their structures and properties

conservation protection and care of an animal or place

conservationist person who works to preserve habitats and save animals

controversial something that causes people to disagree or argue

deforestation act of removing trees from a wooded area

endangered at risk of dying out

extinct dead; no longer existing

fossil remains or impression of a living thing from long ago

gorge steep, narrow valley

great ape large primate, including the chimpanzee, gorilla, and orangutan

habitat place where an animal makes its home

legacy gift that is left behind for future generations

occupational therapy treatment for people with physical or other disabilities that helps them learn how to lead independent, meaningful lives

paleontology science of learning more about ancient times through finding and studying fossil remains

patrol group of people who watch and guard against enemies

physics science of matter (anything that takes up space and has substance) and energy and their relationship

pneumonia disease that causes inflammation of the lungs and other symptoms

poacher person who illegally hunts and kills animals

population number of a type of animal or people that live in an area

preservation act of keeping something safe

primate member of a group of animals that includes humans, apes, monkeys, and lemurs

rain forest thickly wooded area that receives heavy rain throughout the year

species group of living things that are related to each other

subspecies category of animals in biology that ranks just below a species

tourism industry business of serving those who visit an area for pleasure

vegetation plants that are growing in an area

veterinary science study of caring for and treating animals

zoology scientific study of animal life

Find Out More

Books

Hatkoff, Juliana. *Looking for Miza: The True Story of the Mountain Gorilla Family Who Rescued One of Their Own*. New York: Scholastic, 2008.

Nichols, Michael. *Face to Face with Gorillas*. Washington, D.C.: National Geographic, 2009.

Ottaviani, Jim, and Maris Wicks. *Primates: The Fearless Science of Jane Goodall, Dian Fossey, and Biruté Galdikas*. New York: First Second, 2013.

Websites

www.endangeredspeciesinternational.org
This website provides lots of facts and reveals the many dangers facing mountain gorillas and other species throughout the world.

gorilladoctors.org
Keep up to date on what veterinarians are doing to help mountain gorillas in the wild.

gorillafund.org
This is the website of the Dian Fossey Gorilla Fund International, the group that Fossey herself founded.

ngm.nationalgeographic.com/2008/07/archive/fossey-gorillas-1970/dian-fossey-text
Read Fossey's own words about her initial contacts with the mountain gorillas of Rwanda.

DVDs

The Lost Film of Dian Fossey. New York: Films Media Group, 2010.

Musa Lubega's Life with Mountain Gorillas. Brooklyn, N.Y.: Kunaki, 2007.

Nature: The Gorilla King. New York: Educational Broadcasting Corporation and Tigress Productions, 2008.

Places to Visit

Because mountain gorillas cannot survive for long in captivity, the only place to see these amazing creatures is in their natural habitat. If you are interested in traveling to Africa, here are ideas to help you plan your visit:

African safaris

A company called Natural World Safaris, headquartered in the United Kingdom, offers trips to Africa and Asia to visit the great apes. For more information, visit its website at worldprimatesafaris.com.

Rwanda

Those wanting to visit the gorillas in Rwanda must purchase a permit through the Rwanda Development Board. For more information, visit this group at www.rdb.rw

Uganda

The Uganda Wildlife Authority is the organization in charge of permits in that nation. Visit ugandawildlife.org for more information.

What can I do?

What part of Dian Fossey's mission inspired you? How can you follow in her footsteps and help endangered animals? First, research endangered species in your area. Then talk to local conservationists about how you can help. If you are interested in saving mountain gorillas, you might want to get together with your friends and "adopt" a gorilla. Visit Fossey's Gorilla Fund website or the World Wildlife Organization's site (worldwildlife.org) for more information.

Index